Beyond Male and Female
THE GENDER IDENTITY SPECTRUM

LGBTQ
LIFE

BEYOND MALE AND FEMALE
THE GENDER IDENTITY SPECTRUM

By Anita R. Walker

Mason Crest
Philadelphia • Miami

Mason Crest
450 Parkway Drive, Suite D
Broomall, PA 19008
(866) MCP-BOOK (toll free)
www.masoncrest.com

Printed in the United States of America
First printing
9 8 7 6 5 4 3 2 1
Series ISBN: 978-1-4222-4273-5
Hardcover ISBN: 978-1-4222-4274-2
E-book ISBN: 978-1-4222-7521-4

Cataloging-in-Publication Data is available on file at the Library of Congress.

Developed and Produced by Print Matters Productions, Inc. (www.printmattersinc.com)

Cover and Interior Design by Tim Palin Creative

QR CODES AND LINKS TO THIRD-PARTY CONTENT

CONTENTS

KEY ICONS TO LOOK FOR

WORDS TO UNDERSTAND: These words, with their easy-to-understand definitions, will increase readers' understanding of the text while building vocabulary skills.

SIDEBARS: This boxed material within the main text allows readers to build knowledge, gain insights, explore possibilities, and broaden their perspectives by weaving together additional information to provide realistic and holistic perspectives.

EDUCATIONAL VIDEOS: Readers can view videos by scanning our QR codes, providing them with additional educational content to supplement the text.

TEXT-DEPENDENT QUESTIONS: These questions send the reader back to the text for more careful attention to the evidence presented there.

RESEARCH PROJECTS: Readers are pointed toward areas of further inquiry connected to each chapter. Suggestions are provided for projects that encourage deeper research and analysis.

SERIES GLOSSARY OF KEY TERMS: This back-of-the-book glossary contains terminology used throughout this series. Words found here increase the reader's ability to read and comprehend higher-level books and articles in this field.

I'm so excited that you've decided to pick up this book! I can't tell you how much something like this would have meant to me when I was in high school in the early 2000s. Thinking back on that time, I can honestly say I don't recall ever reading anything positive about the LGBTQ community. And while *Will & Grace* was one of the most popular shows on television at the time, it never made me feel as though such stories could be a reality for me. That's in part why it took me nearly a decade more to finally come out in 2012 when I was 25 years old; I guess I knew so little about what it meant to be LGBTQ that I was never really able to come to terms with the fact that I was queer myself.

But times have changed so much since then. In the United States alone, marriage equality is now the law of the land; conversion therapy has been banned in more than 15 states (and counting!); all 50 states have been served by an openly LGBTQ-elected politician in some capacity at some time; and more LGBTQ artists and stories are being celebrated in music, film, and on television than ever before. And that's just the beginning! It's simply undeniable: *it gets better.*

After coming out and becoming the proud queer person I am today, I've made it my life's goal to help share information that lets others know that they're never alone. That's why I now work for the It Gets Better Project (www.itgetsbetter.org), a nonprofit with a mission to uplift, empower, and connect LGBTQ youth around the globe. The organization was founded in September 2010 when the first It Gets Better video was uploaded to YouTube. The viral online storytelling movement that quickly followed has generated over 60,000 video stories to date, one of the largest collections of LGBTQ stories the world has ever seen.

Since then, the It Gets Better Project has expanded into a global organization, working to tell stories and build communities everywhere. It does this through three core programs:

- **Media.** We continue to expand our story collection to reflect the vast diversity of the global LGBTQ community and to make it ever more accessible to LGBTQ youth everywhere. (See, itgetsbetter.org/stories.)
- **Global.** Through a growing network of affiliates, the It Gets Better Project is helping to equip communities with the knowledge, skills, and resources they need to tell their own stories. (See, itgetsbetter.org/global.)
- **Education.** It Gets Better stories have the power to inform our communities and inspire LGBTQ allies, which is why we're working to share them in as many classrooms and community spaces we can. (See, itgetsbetter.org/education.)

You can help the It Gets Better Project make a difference in the lives of LGBTQ young people everywhere. To get started, go to www.itgetsbetter.org and click "Get Involved." You can also help by sharing this book and the other incredible volumes from the LGBTQ Life series with someone you know and care about. You can also share them with a teacher or community leader, who will in turn share them with countless others. That's how movements get started.

In short, I'm so proud to play a role in helping to bring such an important collection like this to someone like you. I hope you enjoy each and every book, and please don't forget: *it gets better.*

Justin Tindall
Director, Education and
Global Programming
It Gets Better Project

Introduction

All of us are assigned a gender at birth. You are either male or female, according to traditional thinking, based on your genitalia. But what about those of us that don't fit such a simplistic either/or model? What if we see ourselves as neither male nor female, but something different?

Despite what we're taught, gender isn't always determined by genitalia alone. It's entirely possible that a person can be born with female genitalia and yet not identify as female, or be born with male genitalia and not identify as male. It's also possible that a person can be born with either male or female genitalia and choose not to self-identify as any gender at all. Gender is as much a societal creation as it is a biological one. Gender is fluid—not fixed—and each of us should be able to choose our gender identity without fear of judgment from family, friends, or neighbors.

It's easy to confuse gender and sexuality because so often the two are discussed as if they were the same thing. But there is an important difference. Namely, sexuality is an expression of gender. In other words, whom we are attracted to is informed by how we perceive our own gender. Someone born biologically male might not necessarily be sexually attracted to someone born biologically female, or vice versa. Our gender, then, however we might choose to name it, informs our sexuality.

From birth, children are assigned gender roles based on genitalia. For example, boys traditionally are dressed in blue and encouraged to be aggressive, while girls are dressed in pink and taught to be passive. Some cultures have more than the two primary genders and have recognized a third gender since the beginning of their civilization.

In truth, gender is only a word. As humans, we require language to communicate, but it is how you feel inside that matters. The author Kate Bornstein writes about how a new approach to words may lead to a better understanding of the spectrum of gender expression:

Instead of saying that all gender is this or all gender is that, let's recognize that the word gender has scores of meanings built into it. It's an amalgamation of bodies, identities, and life experiences, subconscious urges, sensations, and behaviors, some of which develop organically, and others which are shaped by language and culture. Instead of saying that gender is any one single thing, let's start describing it as a holistic experience.

Hateful speech is protected in our society, but that too is only words. The words hurt, but they do not define you if you don't let them. The author Nikki Sex writes about words and the pain they cause:

Strange how mean words can return to one's thoughts, years after they've been callously thrown at you. They replay in your mind, spiking a sense of remembered pain. Nasty name calling can be an ugly memory that stabs unexpectedly—not unlike a nightmare where you wake up crying.

   Sticks and stones, may break your bones—yet, cruel names can hurt you.

Words can be used as weapons. But remember, they can also be used to express love and adoration. It is up to all of us not to allow the bad to overshadow the good in the world. The truth is that we, as humans, have much more in common than not.

   Throughout this book, you will read personal stories from people who are dealing with gender identity beyond male and female. Each has a story to share about how they've questioned, explored, and, finally, reached a place of self-acceptance on their own terms. They've stepped outside of the traditional male–female expectations and found comfort in rich and varied nonconforming gender identities.

   Performer Miley Cyrus describes her path to gender self-expression:

It wasn't that I wanted to *not* be a girl. I didn't want to be a boy. I kind of wanted to be nothing. I don't relate to what people would say defines a girl or a boy, and I think that's what I had to understand: Being a girl … it's the box that I get put into. The definition is what I don't like. The box is what I don't like. It's the [stereotype of] weakness, and the vulnerability. . . . I'm strong. As you get older, I think I just started to celebrate it, because I learned more about what women really are. . . . But it took me a while to get like that.

It can take a while for most of us to "get like that," as she puts it. But one of the first steps is to find your voice and, from there, determine for yourself who you are, whether that falls within the traditional genders or beyond.

We are all assigned a gender at birth.

1

BEYOND STEREOTYPES

DEMOGRAPHIC: *A specific sector of a population, sometimes identified for the purposes of marketing or political targeting.*

NON–BINARY: *A broad category for gender identities that are not exclusively masculine or feminine, male or female, also known as genderqueer. Non-binary people may embrace a combination of masculinity and femininity, or neither, as their expressed gender.*

STEREOTYPE: *A widely held belief about a marginal part of any given population. Stereotyping is oversimplifying a preconception of a group of people.*

All of us are exposed to **stereotypes** every day. They surround us from the ads we see the moment we wake up and check our phones, and all throughout the rest of the day. We're told that women are soft, passive, objects of sexual desire, while men are ambitious, rugged, and success oriented. These are the so-called societal norms we've all grown up with, norms that may be challenged by an ever-changing culture, yet ultimately firmly in place.

But what about those of us who don't fit these pervasive sexual stereotypes that tell us what is considered normal? Are we automatically abnormal if we don't relate to these stereotypes? Some biological females prefer dressing in male-tailored suits, while some biological men choose to go about their lives in dresses. Does gender nonconformity, then, deserve to be castigated because it defies sexual stereotypes embraced by our culture?

There are a host of misinformed assumptions regarding gender identities, including the belief that girls are more sensitive than boys;

We are exposed to stereotypes every day.

Stereotypes related to gender expectations start at birth.

boys are more aggressive than girls and compete to win; and that girls compete for attention. The gender stereotypes are endless. As with any stereotype, there may be truth to our assumptions, but these stereotypes should not be held as legitimate and applicable to all regardless.

Stereotypes around gender expectations start at birth. One is deemed either a boy or a girl, and from there, life unfolds according to that gender. Stereotypes get reinforced continuously through our environment, including home life, the classroom, and the mass media. Television shows and movies target a **demographic**, which is usually gender-based and intended to affirm gender assumptions. But more and more people are beginning to understand that gender is beyond a sexual binary.

For instance, Facebook allows users to choose from among 58 gender identities, including genderfluid, female to male, male to female, cisgender male, and cisgender female, to name a few. One Facebook user immediately changed gender and personal pronouns when the options became available. "I was so excited about that," said the twenty-year-old college student, who identifies as genderqueer, non-binary, and prefers the pronoun *they*. "It makes me feel finally like my identity is being validated by someone other than myself. We live in a culture that says that you're a boy or a girl or a man or a woman, and there's nothing else in-between."

The process of finding oneself starts at home. Parents want what is best for their children. But while they must guide their children through life, the path is never perfect. More often than not, it is this desire to make the child's path easier that prompts parents to attempt to correct the course when their child strays from cultural norms. Parents, as the primary source of a child's information, profoundly affect gender roles during a child's formative years. They choose how restrictive or permissive to be in their child's development. While the freedom to express who we are within our family is ideal, it is not always available. Parents are people, too, and they are not immune to society's pressures as they are bombarded with gendered stereotypes just as we all are.

Beyond the home, the larger community or culture plays a significant role in any child's ability to realize their true self. Societal norms insist on treating a child according to their gender. Baby showers are a great example. Pink for girls; blue for boys. The new trend of gender-neutral parties has helped to spur the market for non-gender-coded onesies, toys, and room decor. Non-traditional approaches to gender in parenting and marketing are becoming more common.

Well-meaning parents often push their sons toward sports without asking what their sons truly want.

TRADITIONAL GENDER ROLES

The gender-awareness journey is ongoing. It is not easy to go against a system set up before birth. The boxes get checked, and pink or blue are the chosen colors.

Addressing the male stereotype as a whole is as dizzying experience. Sports are a big one. Boys are expected to play sports. Well-meaning parents often push their sons toward football, baseball, basketball—any sport will do—without asking what their son truly wants.

The actor Tom Phelan, known for his role on the popular TV show *The Fosters*, identifies as **non-binary** and uses *they* as the chosen

Some people think girls are supposed to wear dresses with frills.

pronoun. Phelan is an inspiring exception, but an exception nonetheless. Society still expects males to behave like men are expected, namely being aggressive, outspoken about their likes and dislikes, looking a certain way, withholding emotions, and carrying themselves as "men" at all times.

The singer Sam Smith was labeled gay for the majority of his career, but he says he "feels just as much woman as I am man." His self-awareness has allowed him to feel far more comfortable in his skin, and his music has flourished as a result. Having come to grips with his true self, Smith has been able to write lyrics straight from the heart. Smith risked his career by bucking traditional gender roles, but his songs are full of hope.

And just like boys, girls must navigate their own set of gender expectations. Girls are expected to be emotional and concerned with their looks, to read romance novels, to watch rom-coms and trauma-drama television shows, and to carry themselves as "ladies." But who says every girl must be exactly alike? Gender nonconforming actor Ruby Rose, known for her role in *Orange Is the New Black,* is having none of it. Rose states, "I am very genderfluid and feel more like I wake up every day sort of gender neutral." Just because some people think girls are supposed to don dresses with frills and blush at flirtations doesn't mean that that is who you are or what you must do.

Within households, children are already seeing their parents step out of traditional gender roles.

HUMAN RIGHTS—STEREOTYPES PERSIST

The framework of international human rights law, at least in theory, is supposed to protect people from harmful stereotyping. It is a human right, recognized by the United Nations, not to be hindered by simply having male or female genitalia. It is intended to protect people from discrimination by sex in all areas of life. But in reality, men, women, and those in between still face disproportionate discrimination if they are part of a marginalized group. If someone is in a minority or indigenous group, has disabilities, is of a lower economic status, or has non-traditional sexual or gender identities, then they are more

THE EQUALIZATION OF GENDER BEGINS AT HOME

Full equality for everyone is a goal we've not yet reached. But within households, children are already seeing their parents step out of traditional gender roles. The reduction in stereotyped gender roles in the home is resulting in children raised with views of gender roles that are very different from those of earlier generations.

The idea that there are distinct roles for men and women is slowly but surely being changed. Increasing numbers of stay-at-home dads and breadwinner moms are a good example of this. "The era of male dominance is coming to an end," Reihan Salam stated in his article, "The Death of Macho," published in *Foreign Policy*. Indeed, Salam's quote points to a progressive movement well underway.

As women continue to challenge the stereotypical female role, men will have to adjust their own understanding of gender roles. "Boys will need to strike a better balance between separation and connection, domin-ance, and submission," Dan Kindlon explains in his article "Descent of Men" on gender role changes. "As their sisters have, boys will need to incorporate elements of both their father's and mother's into their personalities." Kindlon observes, "Better education and higher earnings provide a financial safety net for women today that dependent housewives in the 1950s didn't have." The timely observation points to the fact that both sexes have an unprecedented opportunity to consider roles beyond biological gender.

Women continue to challenge the stereotypical female roles.

The rights of people who do not fit cookie-cutter gender roles are still at risk.

Depression is a very real risk for gender nonconforming people.

likely to be treated with less regard in all aspects of life. In some ways, in-your-face intentional negative bias is easier to address than generalized discrimination.

In spite of advances, the rights of people who do not fit cookie-cutter gender roles are still at risk. Among the challenges they face are access to adequate affordable health care, comfortable living space, education, family and marriage, and protections against gender-based violence. The law does not provide adequate protections, and persistent stereotypes make many feel as though they are on the outskirts of society for not conforming to society's expectations of what it is to be male and female. It is beyond the two genders, and not between, that some people find themselves, despite what they are taught is normal.

DO NOT BECOME A STATISTIC

The discrimination against genderqueer individuals is pervasive and perhaps helps explain why some individuals are cautious, or even closeted, when it comes to coming out as gender nonconforming. Forty-one percent of genderqueer teens attempt suicide, according to the National Gay and Lesbian Task Force and National Center for Transgender Equality. By comparison, the average of teens for the rest of American society is only 4.6 percent. The vast difference in the rate of suicide and attempted suicide is a stark reminder that stereotypes have terrible consequences. Depression is a very real risk for gender-nonconforming people, and they must fight with all their strength not to become a statistic. Find support, whether online or in your community. You are not alone.

Tyler Ford, a writer and contestant on *The Glee Project* in 2012, took a self-reflective journey in order not to be a statistic. The search for his true self led Ford to discover his non-binary feelings and his queer identity. The journey took time and worked much like putting a puzzle together. Ford described the experience in his blog, "Strangers are desperate to know what genitalia I have":

> I have been out as an agender, or genderless, person for about a year now. To me, this simply means having the freedom to exist as a person without being confined by the limits of the western gender binary. I wear what I want to wear and do what I want to do, because it is absurd to limit myself to certain activities, behaviors or expressions based on gender. People don't know what to make of me when they see me, because they feel my features contradict one another. They see no room for the curve of my hips to coexist with my facial

It is absurd to limit yourself to certain activities, behaviors, or expressions based on gender.

Breaking out of the boxes that stereotypes try to put us in is a process.

hair; they desperately want me to be someone they can easily categorize. My existence causes people to question everything they have been taught about gender, which in turn inspires them to question what they know about themselves, and that scares them.

It Gets Better
Elliot Fletcher of The Fosters

BREAKING STEREOTYPES: A HOW-TO GUIDE

Breaking out of the boxes that stereotypes try to put us in is a process and not an easy one, but it is possible to break out! Hope is on the horizon as long as people continue to remind, demand, and keep the faith that things are changing for the better.

Here are a few activities you may find helpful in rising above the confinement of gender roles:

1. Research the history of stereotypes that are holding you back. The information will help you to understand where these biases come from. The process will likely lead you to a broad spectrum of positive and negative views across cultures, countries, and belief systems. This knowledge help to lead the way toward understanding yourself and appreciating the obstacles that you or others may face.

2. Engage with your research by asking, what were the preconceptions of the past? How accurate or inaccurate were those beliefs? How accurate are those views now? What aspects are evolving?

3. Consider ways that you might be able to affect preconceptions in a healthy, positive way in both the short and long term. Whether it is in your community or family unit, positive communication goes a long way, even if it begins in small ways.

4. Knowing oneself is essential for a healthy life and a loving heart. Everyone is unique. Everyone comes to their empowerment using different methods. Whether it is as an advocate in your school or community, exercising your true voice gives you the power to advocate for yourself as well. Each person must come up with their own ways of rising above preconceived notions. It might not always be easy, but it's a process and a journey that will empower you.

Knowing oneself is essential for a healthy life and a loving heart.

TEXT-DEPENDENT QUESTIONS

1. What is the generalized term that addresses marketing targeting?

2. Which international body declares freedom from gender discrimination to be a human right?

3. What are some of society's stereotypical male behaviors?

RESEARCH PROJECTS

1. Make a list of the gender expectations that bother you the most.

2. Choose a person you admire from the past or present, famous or not. How do they inspire you in your own life?

2

GENDER FLUIDITY

WORDS TO UNDERSTAND

ANTHROPOLOGIST: *Someone who studies cultures and societies. They also explore the evolution of humans' biological and physiological characteristics.*

GENDER FLUIDITY: *Not identifying as a fixed gender but flowing between male and female roles and identities.*

PANSEXUAL: *Referring to someone who is open to being sexual with anyone regardless of a person's sex or gender identification or sexual orientation.*

Anthropologists have tracked **gender fluidity** to the beginning of humankind. It is far from a new concept in the human experience, and that fact can be of great comfort to someone who is grappling with gender identity. In his bestselling memoir, *Symptoms of Being Human*, Jeff Garvin tells how important it was to discover that he was not alone in his feelings:

> At some point during my research, I came across the term 'gender fluid.' Reading those words was a revelation. It was like someone tore a layer of gauze off the mirror, and I could see myself clearly for the first time. There was a name for what I was. It was a thing. Gender fluid. Sitting there in front of my computer—like I am right now—I knew I would never be the same. I could never go back to see it the old way; I could never go back to not knowing what I was.

Garvin's experience is shared by many people. Discovering the existence of genderfluid people like you is exhilarating. While some people may feel it's easier to go through life without asking yourself

Discovering the existence of genderfluid people like you is exhilarating.

questions about sexuality and gender, the ability to look into a mirror and know who is looking back is priceless.

Identifying as genderfluid or non-binary may also include sexual preference. **Pansexual** is a term of sexual preference often adopted by those on the gender spectrum. Pansexuality feels most comfortable for these people because in choosing not to identify as a particular gender, they do not have "a type." Although sexuality and gender are not directly related, in practice there can be some overlap.

Identifying as genderfluid or non-binary may also include sexual preference

Your gender identity is separate and independent of who you are attracted to.

GENDER FLUIDITY AND SEXUALITY

The actress Natasha Negovanlis tells her fans, "How you identify or what you prefer in the bedroom does not define your goals, dreams, or interests, and has no bearing on who you are as a human being. You don't need to dress or behave a certain way because of your sexual orientation if you don't want to. Trust that there are groups and resources out there that will support you no matter what. I know that I certainly appreciate all of my fans equally!"

Androgynous people enjoy the freedom of not following conventional roles.

Negovanlis raises a very important issue, namely, that gender ("how you identify") is not the same as sexuality ("what you prefer in the bedroom"). People often confuse the two even though they are separate and independent of one another. For example, on any given day, you might identify as genderless or multiple genders. You might also love another person who identifies as heterosexual or even asexual. The possibilities are boundless. But the point is that your gender identity is separate and independent of who you are attracted to.

People who identify as genderfluid may also want to come off as androgynous, not conforming to either male or female traditional roles. They may prefer to present themselves in public as androgynous

Genderfluid pronouns can be tricky.

by styling their hair or choosing to dress a certain way. Androgynous people enjoy the freedom of not following conventional roles.

Genderfluid pronouns can be tricky. Gender is deeply embedded in language, so much so that proper names and pronouns are an important issue for genderfluid people. The more neutral *They* and *them* are certainly an improvement over *he* and *she*. But genderfluid activists have also introduced a host of original pronouns. These include *ey*, *ze*, *co*, *hir*, and *sie*. Similarly, the title *Mx* is used by some as a replacement for *Mr.* and *Ms.*

Unisex names are standard for those who identify as genderqueer.

Author, artist, activist, and songwriter Ashley Jay Brockwell is genderfluid. In the article "International Non-Binary People's Day: Thinking Outside the 'M/F' Box," Brockwell writes,

> For me, discovering the term "non-binary" was both a revelation and a relief. It created a space in which I felt safe to admit I don't always feel like a woman. . . . In fact, I very rarely feel like a woman. . . . Oh, all right, if I'm completely honest with myself, the truth is that I'm *not* a woman. I started coming out as non-binary in November 2017, changing from a very feminine name to the unisex name Ashley.

Unisex names are standard for those who identify as genderqueer. Although your parents, teachers, and friends may feel that you are challenging them by changing to a gender-neutral name, in time they may understand why. Changing your name to fit your personality can be a healthy step on your journey to self-discovery.

Fighting Gender Binary Stereotypes

- Gender fluidity is not a mental or physical illness. You have recent medical and mental health research on your side.
- The way people express their gender varies from culture to culture. It was once called a mental illness to not abide by gender roles in our culture. Some cultures have long recognized a third gender beyond male and female.
- You might take on gender expressions that are new to both you and your inner circle of friends and family. Keep in mind that everyone's experience is unique. Clear and positive communication only allows your friends and family to get to know the real you.
- Your gender identity is a foundation that you will continue to build throughout your lifetime.
- The support of family, friends, and community is no small thing. If you are fortunate enough to have that, you will have a safe environment in which to flourish. If you don't have it, keep looking.

The way people express their gender varies from culture to culture.

Real communication only happens when minds are open.

YOU ARE YOUR BEST ADVOCATE

Whether you advocate for yourself or others, it's important to remember that no two people are alike. You may prefer one set of pronouns, while someone else who identifies the same way uses a different vocabulary. Some feel more comfortable in the center of the spectrum between man and woman. Others move more fluidly between the two genders. When a person asks you about your gender, take into account their beliefs and why they are asking. If the person is a stranger, you might want to use

It Gets Better
Emily Robinson from "Eighth Grade"

Keep up with new research and writings about gender role issues.

No one is expecting you to be all things to all people.

simple language and find common ground that you both understand for a safe conversation. The same applies if you are advocating for others. Real communication only happens when minds are open, and you're speaking the same language.

Never stop educating yourself. Keep up with new research, writings about gender role issues, and the latest statistics. It not only helps with your own discovery, but also gives you the tools to stand up for yourself when speaking to someone who does not understand gender nonconformity.

Other tips for self-advocacy:

- Check in with yourself on a regular basis. You cannot advocate for yourself if you are not mentally prepared for all possibilities.
- Stay up to date on changes in laws, at both the state and federal levels. It's important to know your rights and how to defend yourself against injustice.
- Get involved! Many cities have LGBTQ centers and community activist groups.
- Start slowly. Find your comfort level, and build from there. No one is expecting you to be all things to all people.

TEXT-DEPENDENT QUESTIONS

1. Why is *pansexual* a preferred term of sexual orientation for many genderfluid people?

2. What are some examples of non-gendered pronouns?

3. Are gender and sexuality the same thing?

RESEARCH PROJECT

Research traditional gender roles and contrast and compare them with the spectrum of genderqueer identities. How has gender identity evolved?

3

WORDS MATTER

FOCUSING ON
SEX PARTS MA
YOU
THE PERVER

I'M NOT A
BOY OR A
GIRL
WHERE DO
I PEE?!

WORDS TO UNDERSTAND

CISGENDER: Referring to someone who identifies with the gender assigned to them at birth. *Cis* is a shorter version of cisgender.

GENDER POLICING: Forcing people to conform to traditional male and female gender expression, stemming from the belief that only two genders exist.

INTERSEX: A non-derogatory term referring to a combination of chromosomes, hormones, and genitalia that is both male and female. Intersex people were once known as hermaphrodites or hermaphroditic, but these terms are now considered derogatory.

TRANSGENDER: Referring to persons who live their life as a gender different from the one assigned to them at birth.

Male, female, girl, boy, he, and *she* are just words, but they matter. Labels and pronouns and the expectations that come with them often keep people from questioning the gender box they are put in at birth. The box begins with the checkmark on a birth certificate and carries over to nearly every official form we fill out.

Words have power. They can help someone feel comfortable about who they are, but they can also make someone feel bad about who they are. Not everyone will get pronouns or identification right every time, but the important thing is to try. Learning and using new words to express non-binary gender identity may feel strange at first, but by doing so, you are demonstrating respect for genderfluid people.

Pronouns are the perfect example. The pronouns a person prefers are a personal choice, and using a person's pronouns of choice shows consideration and respect. While many people identify as genderfluid or non-binary, each may prefer different pronouns. Some might use

they, *them*, and *their*, while others prefer *ey*, *ze*, *co*, *hir*, or *sie*. Similarly, the term *Mx* has been adopted by some as a replacement for Mr. and Ms. If you are in a safe space and place in your life, it is perfectly polite to ask others to use your pronouns of choice. Not only is it polite, but it can also turn an awkward conversation into a positive, shared experience.

The writer Jill Soloway, of the hit TV show *Transparent*, who prefers the pronouns *they* and *their* and came out as gender non-binary in 2017, began their journey as a daughter of a **transgender** parent.

The pronouns a person prefers are a personal choice.

Gender is like a Rubik's Cube with one hundred squares per side.

Soloway's writing and show running for *Transparent* was an eye-opening experience, helping them to realize that they are gender neutral. While Soloway's identifying as gender non-binary was new to them, their feelings that led to that decision had always been there.

For people like Soloway, who do not identify as male or female but still want to be spoken about in a sentence, the use of the pronouns *they* and *them* is one of the more straightforward solutions that have been put forward in English. True, these pronouns are traditionally thought of as plural, and their usage does not always fit accepted rules of grammar, but in an imperfect world, it is one of the best ways to refer to a person without implying an assumed gender.

The complexity of gender can be better understood by picturing a Rubik's Cube, according to author and activist Sam Killerman:

> Gender is like a Rubik's Cube with one hundred squares per side, and every time you twist it to take a look at another angle, you make it that much harder a puzzle to solve. The end result of fiddling and moving the hypothetical cube is a metaphor for reaching absolute equality when the colors align. It takes most people ages to finish a Rubik's Cube, if ever. Equality will come faster than a mind-bending activity.

The famous children's author Lorin Morgan-Richards delves into what he believes the future holds for consumers, "One day stores will no longer have gender classifications. Instead, the consumer decides how and what they want, rather than the social engineering of corporations. The concept of gender will be extinct." Morgan-Richards believes that capitalism and gender will catch up with one another eventually, but that is going to take time.

Having talked quite a bit about people who identify as genderfluid, it's important to note that not everyone is comfortable being different. Wanting to be part of a group is a normal human instinct. People who choose to identify as either male or female in accordance with the gender they were assigned at birth are known as **cisgender**. The truth, however, is that even cisgender people experience fluidity of gender, albeit not as dramatically as those who identify as non-binary.

TV producer Jill Soloway, who has wrestled with the complexities of gender identity and its expression, points out that gender expression is independent of a person's particular anatomy:

> I think it's more about the binary, the masculine and feminine. There will always be incredibly masculine people and completely feminine people, but that has nothing to do with people's bodies, whether they have a penis or vagina. And besides those two poles, there's also a place in the middle, the non-binaries, the people who don't register as one or the other. I'm happy

There will always be incredibly masculine people and completely feminine people.

Words do hurt and sometimes inflict long-term damage.

to speak on behalf of women and on behalf of feminism. But I notice when people see me as non-binary, I get treated more as a human being.

Intersex describes people who have anatomical aspects that are both male and female. The variations among intersex people include genitalia, breasts, and ovaries and/or production of both male and female hormones. While the term *hermaphrodite* was once used to describe someone who has both male and female chromosomes, hormones, and genitalia, *intersex* is now the accepted word.

In Anne Fausto-Sterling's essay "The Five Sexes: Why Male and Female Are Not Enough," Fausto-Sterling argues,

> The existence of intersex people, individuals possessing a combination of male and female sexual characteristics, who are seen as deviations from the norm and who frequently undergo coercive surgery at a very young age in order to maintain the two-gender system, challenges the standards of gender binaries and puts into question society's role in constructing gender.

"Sticks and stones may break my bones, but words will never hurt me," the old saying goes. But the truth is that words do hurt and sometimes inflict long-term damage. Remember, though, hurt feelings and hateful words do not define you or anyone else. Learn from words that hurt as much and those that make you smile. Rejection is not your fault. Live your truth, regardless of the label society uses.

WORDS WILL HURT YOU—HOW TO DEAL WITH IT

The LGBTQ community is comprised of as many gender and sexual identities as there are LGBTQ people. Despite sharing a broad queer identity, the community is incredibly varied in terms of self-identity.

C. N. Lester, a genderfluid person, who was profiled in a magazine article titled "None of the Above," is an example of how gender nonconforming people are becoming more visible in the mainstream media:

> Lester, who as a child hated being called a girl but never felt quite like a "man trapped in a woman's body," came out as transgender 15 years ago. As an umbrella term, the word *transgender* refers to those whose sense of their gender differs from what is expected based on the sex characteristics with which they are born. The transgender stereotype, at least in mainstream culture, is a person who identifies as the "other" gender and switches from a masculine appearance to a feminine

The LGBTQ community is comprised of as many gender and sexual identities as there are LGBTQ people.

Homophobia persists, even among the educated.

one, or vice versa. That narrative has grown increasingly familiar in recent years. And the public visibility of transgender people has taken off: Colleges have created gender-neutral bathrooms and transgender awareness programs; the award-winning Amazon series *Transparent* centers on protagonist Mort, who comes out as Maura late in life; and transgender actress Laverne Cox has illuminated both the Netflix drama *Orange Is the New Black* and, last June, a *Time* magazine cover trumpeting "The Transgender Tipping Point."

It Gets Better
Encouraging Letters to LGBTQ+
Students: 48 Hours of Love

Do not argue with someone who has made up their mind about you, but try to give everyone the benefit of the doubt. The difference between educating and engaging in an argument becomes evident pretty quickly. Advocacy comes in different ways. Situations will arise where you will be able to use your self-advocacy to help others get out of hurtful or uncomfortable situations. Here are some tips for engaging with and educating people who spout hurtful speech:

- The word *queer* can be used in both positive and negative connotations. Always consider who is using the term and their intended meaning. It can be used to hurt but also to show pride in how someone chooses to identify.
- Homophobia persists, even among the educated. Hurtful actions and words, unfortunately, are part of life. People even fear bisexual men and women, which is referred to as *biphobia*. (The word *phobia* means an exaggerated or irrational fear.) Sometimes that fear is so deeply rooted that the person is not even aware of it. But that does not mean we cannot try to change minds. Ignorant bullies should never be allowed to make you question your worth as a human being.
- People who take it upon themselves to police traditional gender roles sometimes lack information, and sometimes they simply choose to remain narrow-minded. Regardless of the root, in the end, forgiveness of even the most hateful speech can be liberating for you on the path to your true self. The inspirational quote author Shannon L. Alder offers this sound advice: "You need to forgive people you don't understand; if not, try to understand people you want to forgive."

GENDER POLICE GENERALIZE THE OTHER

Gender policing stems from the belief that only two genders exist and that everyone should conform to those roles. The most prevalent form of gender policing is directed at the transgender community. The battle over gendered bathroom access in schools and other public

The most prevalent form of gender policing is directed at the transgender community.

Don't worry if you get someone's gender wrong.

places, which has erupted into the news in recent years, is one of the most blatant examples of gender policing. But the tide is slowly turning as genderless restrooms enter the mainstream. Advocacy groups file lawsuits on a regular basis for equal access on behalf of transgender and gender nonconforming people.

Gender policing also shows up in countless less dramatic ways, such as criticizing people for the way they dress, walk, and speak because it doesn't conform to masculine and feminine stereotypes.

Live your truth, regardless of the labels society uses.

People's attitudes are slowly changing, but it always hurts to be put down for being who you are.

PREFERRED PRONOUNS

The pronouns a person chooses to be known by are a matter of personal preference. Always ask. It might feel awkward, but non-binary individuals are often more than happy to tell you. Don't worry if you get someone's gender wrong. We all make mistakes. The important thing is to note when you're corrected, and try not to repeat the mistake.

TEXT-DEPENDENT QUESTIONS

1. What visual metaphors have been used by celebrities and academic theorists to make their journey relatable and easier to understand for all ages?

2. What is gender policing?

3. What is the best way to find out which pronouns a person prefers?

RESEARCH PROJECTS

1. Make lists of words that can be used to harm and words that can be used to nurture. See whether you can turn the negative words into positive ones.

2. Search online for community outreach programs for LGBTQ individuals. Local schools and even Chambers of Commerce increasingly sponsor programs for young people who identify as anything other than cisgender. If you can't find a supportive group that appeals to you, consider starting one either at school or in the community.

4

IT'S NOT NEW

WORDS TO UNDERSTAND

GLAAD: *Formerly known as the Gay & Lesbian Alliance Against Defamation, GLAAD is a non-profit organization founded by LGBTQ people in the media. The media watchdog organization keeps stats, updates research, and advocates for a broad spectrum of people.*

HIJRA: *A male in Indian culture who prefers to dress and take on feminine characteristics. The hijra face their own struggles within a now-hidden caste system in India.*

MUXES: *A biological male in Mexico's Oaxaca state, who identifies as female or genderless. Muxe is also a slang term meaning female or weakling in some areas of Mexico. It is pronounced "moo-shey."*

WARIA: *A biological male in Indonesia who identifies as female. Dating back to the 19th century, they are considered a third gender in their country.*

It might come as a surprise to learn that some Native American tribes celebrated a diversity of gender identities. They called those with a combination of masculine and feminine qualities "two-spirits." Considered special, Two-Spirits were revered and respected by the community. When the European colonists arrived in North America, they brought their gender biases with them. Among the many disruptions of traditional cultures that they caused was the condemnation of Two-Spirits.

Today, the way we view gender fluidity is evolving. **GLAAD** reports that 12 percent of millennials identify as transgender or gender nonconforming, which is significantly more than previous generations. That's largely the result of education, political advocacy,

Today, the way we view gender fluidity is evolving.

and a greater awareness of gender nonconforming people, especially in the entertainment world.

One recent example of positive change comes from India, which recently granted **hijra** legal recognition of whatever gender they choose. Many anthropologists believe that hijra, men who take on feminine characteristics and clothing, have been around for thousands of years—historical documents include the term *third nature*. The legal protections are an important step as the hijra have faced discrimination and violence in modern Indian society.

Many anthropologists believe that hijra have been around for thousands of years.

The word *gender* has scores of meaning built into it.

In *Gender Outlaws: The Next Generation*, transgender author Kate Bornstein provides valuable insight into how gender can be viewed across cultures:

> Instead of saying that all gender is this or all gender is that, let's recognize that the word *gender* has scores of meaning built into it. It's an amalgamation of bodies, identities, and life experiences, subconscious urges, sensations, and behaviors, some of which develop organically, and others which are shaped by language and culture. Instead of saying that gender is any one single thing, let's start describing it as a holistic experience.

There is a rise in public awareness of transgender and gender nonconforming people.

Literature and Language

Although the rise in public awareness of transgender and gender nonconforming people is a hopeful sign, literature demonstrates that transgender and gender nonconforming people have been in the public eye for decades.

1. *The Left Hand of Darkness* by Ursula K. LeGuin: The science fiction novel follows genderless, androgynous, and intersexed characters throughout a foreign world.

2. *Dangerous Space* by Kelley Eskridge: A collection of stories that have been called "Richly imagined, moving, and very sexy . . . will make you rethink all the categories you thought you knew."

3. *The Turbulent Term of Tyke Tiler* by Gene Kemp: The young adult book follows Tyke Tiler, whose gender is never referred to directly but is hinted throughout the story. The reader has the freedom to see Tyke Tiler as genderless until the finale.

4. *Sphinx* by Anne Garréta (trans. Emma Ramadan): The recently translated French novel follows a love story between two people without gender pronouns and markers. The release of the translated version makes available to English readers a love story without gendered protagonists.

5. *Days Without End* by Sebastian Barry: The main character escapes the potato famine in Ireland by migrating to America. The protagonist dresses as a female when entertaining and carries a soldier kit as he fights in two different wars for a country that saved him.

Gender roles have always been culturally specific. Some cultures are rigid on gender, insisting on traditional male and female genders and their corresponding identities, while others are more accommodating, allowing for three and even up to five genders to choose from. Still other cultures don't embrace any gender at all, preferring androgyny. Let's look at how some cultures approach gender identities.

Gender roles have always been culturally specific.

NOTHING NEW: A BRIEF SURVEY OF NON-BINARY GENDERS

Indonesia has long recognized a third gender. Males who identify as female are referred to as **waria**. Yet, the recognition of waria is not the same as acceptance. According to Human Rights Watch, those who identify as a waria face legal discrimination and threats from religious extremists.

In contrast, the native Zapotec population in the Mexican state of Oaxaca, cherishes those who are born male but see themselves as female or even genderless. They refer to the genderqueer as **muxes**. Gender fluidity is considered a blessing or a sign of good luck within families. The acceptance and joy that people show to the third gender, however, is specific to the region. Other areas of Mexico do not share the sentiment.

Following the same cultural thread, Samoan culture refers to males who identify as females or genderless as *fa'afafine*. The BBC reports that 1 to 5 percent of Samoans identify as fa'afafine. An annual beauty pageant held specifically for fa'afafines is a public celebration of their third gender.

Even in cultures that accept a third gender, life is not easy for the gender nonconforming. In *The Samoa Observer*, Siliva'ai Luamanuvae, who identifies as fa'afafine, describes his life:

The native Zapotec population honors those who are born male but see themselves as female or even genderless.

People are different with how they express themselves. For me, doing my hair this way and wearing what I feel like wearing brings me happiness. This is the style I am comfortable with and I don't want to change in any way. I have grown accustomed to styling myself like this and I have no shame in it. As I grew up in my household, the only thing I knew was to respect others. My parents never neglected me or went against any of my choices in life. They let me live my life peacefully as a fa'afafine; the only person I was afraid of was my brother. He was the only one who would force me to stop acting and dressing like a girl. Other than that, my life has been OK and free.

In Hawaii, the *māhū*, the name taken by their culture's third gender, once were revered as healers, caretakers, and teachers. But when Hawaii was colonized by the British in the 19th century, the attitude toward the māhū changed drastically. American settlers, arriving in the 1800s, brought intolerance and Christian religious dogma to the islands. The māhū went from revered to rebuked in the name of the Christians' god. Wong-Kalu, who identifies as māhū, told Al Jazeera: "Our own culture is used against

Even in cultures that accept a third gender, life is not easy for the gender nonconforming.

It Gets Better
Five Videos You Should See

us. The māhū are denigrated and disrespected because of the imposition of foreign ideology."

"Māhū is the expression of the third self," Kaumakaiwa Kanaka'ole, a Native Hawaiian activist and performer explained. "It is not a gender, it's not an orientation, it's not a sect, it's not a particular demographic, and it's definitely not a race. It is simply an expression of the third person as it involves the individual. When you find that place in yourself to acknowledge both male and female aspects within and accept the capacity to embrace both … that is where the māhū exists, and true liberation happens."

These are just a few examples of third genders around the world. They have long existed and been recognized in both Western and Eastern cultures. Throughout history, third genders have been accepted and even revered in their societies. As our own culture moves forward in its re-examination of gender assumptions, these examples can lead the way.

Barbara J. Risman, a professor of sociology at The University of Illinois at Chicago, ponders gender stereotypes throughout history in an academic article for *American Sociological Review*, *Gender & Society*, "There's a part of me that wonders if we didn't have such strong stereotypes about what you had to be to be considered an appropriate man or woman, whether or not more people might be comfortable in those categories."

American settlers, arriving to Hawaii in the 1800s, brought intolerance to the islands.

Beyond Male and Female • The Gender Identity Spectrum

Throughout history, third genders have been accepted and even revered in their societies.

Some cultures are more accommodating, allowing for three and even up to five genders to choose from.

TEXT-DEPENDENT QUESTIONS

1. What are men who identify as women called in Indonesia?

2. What are men who identify as women called in India?

3. What is the Native American name for a third-gender identity?

RESEARCH PROJECT

Research a society that recognizes a third-gender identity. How would it feel to live in that society?

5

An Ongoing Conversation

CONFLICT: *A serious disagreement or argument (noun); to be incompatible or clash with (verb).*

GENDERQUEER: *Someone who does not fit conventional gender roles. Genderqueer individuals may identify as both, neither, or a combination of male and female genders.*

GENERATION: *People born and living at about the same time, whose attitudes and values were shaped by their shared experiences.*

Consider that at this very moment, four generations of people, ranging in age from zero to over 100, live in and contribute to the world we live in. Each generation has a different perspective on the

Each generation has a different perspective on the evolution of genders.

Change and ambiguity are hard for traditionalists to handle.

evolution and progress toward a rainbow of genders. Let's examine the path of each and the experiences that shaped their attitudes toward gender.

TRADITIONALISTS (BORN BETWEEN 1927 AND 1945)

The traditionalist **generation** was strongly influenced by their experience of the Great Depression and its aftermath, as well as World Wars I and II. Traditionalists, like generations before them, are known to adhere to rules, including gender roles, traditional households, and saving each penny for the next economic downfall.

Change and ambiguity are hard for traditionalists to handle. Older adults might tend not to follow trends, and they might not expect a

Baby boomers were shaped by the sexual revolution, the Vietnam War, and Watergate.

change in gender role in a child or grandchild. It's important to keep in mind these limitations when discussing gender with people of this generation.

BABY BOOMERS (BORN BETWEEN 1946 AND 1964)

We have all heard the term *baby boomers*. That generation was shaped by the sexual revolution, the Vietnam War, the fight for civil rights, and Watergate. Many baby boomers share the attitudes of their traditionalist parents when it comes to gender and sexual identity. As adults, baby boomers have tended to carry on the family belief systems of their parents.

Liza J. Anderson's article "One Boomer's New Understanding of Gender Fluidity" illustrates where many people of her generation stand when it comes to gender and sexuality:

> When I was a teenager in the 1970s, I promised myself that in order to remain a vital, full participant in life, I would never get stuck in my ways as I perceived the grown-ups in my life did. I promised I would always be current with new culture, which to me at that time meant fashion, music and slang. Like most of us, I couldn't have imagined the coming changes in our lives and the greater world—that not being outdated and frumpy would mean so much more than wearing what the kids do but is now about being open to understanding new ideas expressed in new language.
>
> Many of our new words have to do with identity and many of those have to do with gender. There is cis-gender, gender neutral, genderqueer, gender nonconforming, genderfluid and one that is new to me: non-binary. During my 23-year hairdressing career, I was lucky to have several gender non-conforming clients who taught me about authenticity and self-acceptance. When I first met each of them in the early 1990s, they didn't have accurate words to describe their gender identity. I also learned that gender identity and sexual

Generation Xers were trailblazers in networking.

orientation are two completely different things. The biological male who wanted to become a woman preferred women and so did the mustached, biological female who identified as a man.

Gender is much more than appearance, but if how we look accurately reflects our inward identity to others, it becomes an affirming loop of expression-reaction that makes us feel at home in our own skin. Whenever I cut my hair extremely short, I feel more energized, as if long hair is a girly lampshade that dims my light.

GENERATION X (BORN BETWEEN 1965 AND 1980)

Generation X runs the gamut of experiences. From the end of the Cold War to the turn of a century and the 9/11 terrorist attacks, those in Generation X have witnessed an evolving America. They were not as active in protests as the generations before and after, but they saw progress toward a greater acceptance of racial, sexual, and gender diversity. Generation Xers were the trailblazers of networking. They began the process of building worldwide communities of like minds.

Generation X witnessed the end of post-World War II prosperity with economic security vanishing in the 1980s. As they came of age, owning a home was not assumed, but both partners in a marriage working outside jobs was.

President Barack Obama offered a glimpse into the thinking of much of his generation, "[G]ender stereotypes affect all of us,

Millennials are tech-savvy beyond anything Generation Xers could have conceived.

regardless of our gender, gender identity, or sexual orientation But I also have to admit that when you're the father of two daughters, you become even more aware of how gender stereotypes pervade our society. . . . You feel the enormous pressure girls are under to look and behave and even think a certain way."

MILLENNIALS (BORN BETWEEN 1981 AND 2000)

You likely identify as a Millennial, or at least others refer to you as one. Millennials are tech-savvy beyond anything Generation X could have conceived. The days of Facebook, Twitter, and Instagram would not be possible without the youngest of generations. Millenials have perfected networking through the various social media platforms. However, they are the first generation to go through mass shooting drills in schools, and in larger cities, terrorist attacks.

Millennials are generally accepting of people who are different from them. The ability to share life experience online has broadened their understanding of cultures and the human condition. The Internet has made possible a sense of community without borders. Television streaming services have made available shows that would have shocked most even a decade ago but that have become popular hits. *Transparent*, for example, was mentioned in previous chapters. A show featuring a transgendered older male lead would not have existed and thrived without continued progression by Millennials.

HOW TO HAVE A CONVERSATION ABOUT GENDER IDENTITY

Most people tend to avoid **conflict**, but conflict does not have to be negative. In fact, when you engage in a healthy way with people who have different belief systems, you can learn from them, and they can learn from you.

Discussing gender identity with someone whose views on the subject are different from yours comes under the heading of "a difficult conversation." Business consultant and Harvard lecturer Douglas Stone offers good advice on how to approach such a discussion, in his book *Difficult Conversations: How to Discuss What Matters Most*:

> Remind yourself that if you think you already understand how someone feels or what they are trying to say, it is a delusion. Remember a time when you were sure you were right and then discovered one little fact that changed everything? There is always more to learn.

THE GAP IN CONVERSATION BETWEEN GENERATIONS

AARP, the American Association of Retired Persons, educates its members about gender and sexuality to promote a more gender-accommodating attitude among older people. For instance, their Web site offers a sample conversation between a Gen X'er (today over 50, in many cases) and a millennial:

Question: Can we be fluid about gender?

Millennial: Yes—we already are! News flash: Male/female/Non-binary. We're all humans!

Gen Xer: I don't even know what *non-binary* means.

Millennial: Really? Since college, I've had several friends who are non-binary. It's where you don't identify as male or female.

Gen Xer: So like transgender?

Millennial: Yes! Trans is where the gender you identify with doesn't match the sex you were assigned at birth. Some people who are trans have surgery, some don't, some take hormones, some don't, some dress in particular ways, some don't — there's a beautiful rainbow spectrum of trans fabulousness.

Gen Xer: Where does sexuality fit into trans identity? This part is confusing to me. Why would a woman become a man and then want to date men?

Millennial: Whoa, whoa, whoa. Gender identity and sexual identity are apples and oranges! Whether I identify as female, male, or non-binary has nothing to do with whom I'm crushing on.

The American Association of Retired Persons educates its members about gender and sexuality.

When you engage in a healthy way with people, you can learn from them.

Here are some tips for making any exchange of conflicting viewpoints more civil and productive.

Show respect for the other person and their opinions, even if you do not feel respected in return. While honest conversations are not a guarantee that you will be friends when the discussion is over, showing respect helps both of you to hear what the other is saying. It's often helpful to start with some aspect of life that you can both agree on. An agreement is a wonderful jumping-off point for an open and honest conversation from which both parties can learn.

Showing respect in a conversation helps both of you to hear what the other is saying.

Open your ears, and remember to close your mouth. Listening is just as important as talking. In a good discussion, both parties learn things they did not know before. If you don't make the effort to really listen to what the other person is saying, you risk simply talking at one another rather than truly engaging. Engaging on a personal level is the key to changing hearts and minds.

Do not avoid conflict. Conversations are how we learn about one another. Disagreements happen, but they don't need to become nasty or personal. If all else fails, you can always end a discussion by saying, "We'll have to agree to disagree."

Expect a positive outcome. Optimism is your friend when entering a conversation where conflict is likely to happen. It is not a debate with winners and losers. The goal of any difficult conversation should be to leave a positive impression and, hopefully, a better mutual understanding.

Correcting people and educating them about gender issues can get tiring.

It Gets Better
A Global Conversation about Russia

The **Genderqueer** activist Jay Culkin (*they, them, their*), who blogs on Bustle.com, confides that correcting people and educating them can get tiring:

> When someone misgenders a gender queer person, it isn't
> as simple as you might think to correct them. You may be
> a lovely, wonderful, and accepting person; that makes you
> one of quite a few. But when a gender queer person doesn't
> know you and doesn't know whether or not you are one of
> those accepting people, correcting people on our names and
> pronouns can lead to uncomfortable situations. Introducing
> yourself as gender queer can make every introduction to
> a new person into a long, educational conversation about
> abstract gender constructs. It gets a little bit boring after a
> while. There are tons of online resources you can turn to (like
> this very article) to get the information you're looking for
> about the gender queer experience.

When genderqueer people explain their gender identity to strangers, they naturally feel wary of a defensive or ignorant response. If you're on the other side of the conversation, a reassuring "you can correct me" or "I don't mind being corrected" is a considerate response. It identifies you as an ally and shows respect.

SHAKING UP STEREOTYPES

We all start our lives with one of two genders assigned at birth. Beyond birth, however, we all grow in different ways. Gender identity for most people is so deeply ingrained that they never question it. That's why it is so difficult to live openly as a person whose gender identity does not fit neatly into the male or female boxes. But remember, you are not alone. There are other people like you, even if you haven't met them yet. You will find people who love and accept you for who you are.

There are other people like you, even if you haven't met them yet.

TEXT-DEPENDENT QUESTIONS

1. Why should healthy conflict not be avoided?

2. What is the best way to approach a potentially heated discussion?

3. Why is listening just as important as talking in a conversation?

RESEARCH PROJECTS

1. What generation are your parents? Have a conversation with them about their generational beliefs.

2. Practice serious discussions until you feel comfortable with the thought of having them with people who are not as safe as family or a friend. For example, if you are planning to come out to a new friend or acquaintance, practice first with a sibling or peer.

Agender (or neutrois, gender neutral, or genderless): Referring to someone who has little or no personal connection with gender.

Ally: Someone who supports equal civil rights, gender equality, and LGBTQ social movements; advocates on behalf of others; and challenges fear and discrimination in all its forms.

Asexual: An adjective used to describe people who do not experience sexual attraction. A person can also be aromantic, meaning they do not experience romantic attraction.

Asexual, or ace: Referring to someone who experiences little or no sexual attraction, or who experiences attraction but doesn't feel the need to act it out sexually. Many people who are asexual still identify with a specific sexual orientation.

Bigender: Referring to someone who identifies with both male and female genders, or even a third gender.

Binary: The belief that such things as gender identity have only two distinct, opposite, and disconnected forms. For example, the belief that only male and female genders exist. As a rejection of this belief, many people embrace a non-binary gender identity. (See **Gender nonconforming.**)

Biphobia: Fear of bisexuals, often based on stereotypes, including inaccurate associations with infidelity, promiscuity, and transmission of sexually transmitted infections.

Bisexual, or bi: Someone who is attracted to those of their same gender as well as to those of a different gender (for example, a woman who is attracted to both women and men). Some people use the word bisexual as an umbrella term to describe individuals that are attracted to more than one gender. In this way, the term is closely related to pansexual, or omnisexual, meaning someone who is attracted to people of any gender identity.

Butch, or masc: Someone whose gender expression is masculine. *Butch* is sometimes used as a derogatory term for lesbians, but it can also be claimed as an affirmative identity label.

Cisgender, or cis: A person whose gender identity matches the gender they were assigned at birth.

Coming out: The process through which a person accepts their sexual orientation and/or gender identity as part of their overall identity. For many, this involves sharing that identity with others, which makes it more of a lifetime process rather than just a one-time experience.

Cross-dresser: While anyone may wear clothes associated with a different sex, the term is typically used to refer to men who occasionally wear clothes, makeup, and accessories that are culturally associated with women. Those men typically identify as heterosexual. This activity is a form of gender expression and not done for entertainment purposes. Cross-dressers do not wish to permanently change their sex or live full-time as women.

Drag: The act of presenting as a different gender, usually for the purpose of entertainment (i.e., drag kings and queens). Many people who do drag do not wish to present as a different gender all of the time.

Gay: Someone who is attracted to those of their same gender. This is often used as an umbrella term but is used more specifically to describe men who are attracted to men.

Gender affirmation surgery: Medical procedures that some individuals elect to undergo to change their physical appearance to resemble more closely the way they view their gender identity.

Gender expression: The external manifestations of gender, expressed through such things as names, pronouns, clothing, haircuts, behavior, voice, and body characteristics.

Gender identity: One's internal, deeply held sense of gender. Some people identify completely with the gender they were assigned at birth (usually male or female), while others may identify with only a part of that gender or not at all. Some people identify with another gender entirely. Unlike gender expression, gender identity is not visible to others.

Gender nonconforming: Referring to someone whose gender identity and/or gender expression does not conform to the cultural or social expectations of gender, particularly in relation to male or female. This can be an umbrella term for many identities, including, but not limited to:

> **Genderfluid:** Someone whose gender identity and/or expression varies over time.

> **Genderqueer (or third gender):** Someone whose gender identity and/or expression falls between or outside of male and female.

Heterosexual: An adjective used to describe people whose enduring physical, romantic, and/ or emotional attraction is to people of the opposite sex. Also **straight**.

Homophobia: Fear of people who are attracted to the same sex. *Intolerance*, *bias*, or *prejudice* are usually more accurate descriptions of antipathy toward LGBTQ people.

Intergender: Referring to someone whose identity is between genders and/or a combination of gender identities and expressions.

Intersectionality: The idea that multiple identities intersect to create a whole that is different from its distinct parts. To understand someone, it is important to acknowledge that each of their identities is important and inextricably linked with all of the others. These can include identities related to gender, race, socioeconomic status, ethnicity, nationality, sexual orientation, religion, age, mental and/or physical ability, and more.

Intersex: Referring to someone who, due to a variety of factors, has reproductive or sexual anatomy that does not seem to fit the typical definitions for the female or male sex. Some people who are intersex may identify with the gender assigned to them at birth, while many others do not.

Lesbian: A woman who is attracted to other women. Some lesbians prefer to identify as gay women.

LGBTQ: Acronym for lesbian, gay, bisexual, transgender, and queer or questioning.

Non-binary and/or genderqueer: Terms used by some people who experience their gender identity and/or gender expression as falling outside the categories of man and woman. They may define their gender as falling somewhere in between man and woman, or they may define it as wholly different from these terms.

Out: Referring to a person who self-identifies as LGBTQ in their personal, public, and/or professional lives.

Pangender: Referring to a person whose identity comprises all or many gender identities and expressions.

Pride: The celebration of LGBTQ identities and the global LGBTQ community's resistance against discrimination and violence. Pride events are celebrated in many countries around the world, usually during the month of June to commemorate the Stonewall Riots that began in New York City in June 1969, a pivotal moment in the modern LGBTQ movement.

Queer: An adjective used by some people, particularly younger people, whose sexual orientation is not exclusively heterosexual (e.g., queer person, queer woman). Typically, for those who identify as queer, the terms *lesbian*, *gay*, and *bisexual* are perceived to be too limiting and/or fraught with cultural connotations that they feel don't apply to them. Some people may use *queer*, or more commonly *genderqueer*, to describe their gender identity and/or gender expression (see **non-binary** and/or **genderqueer**). Once considered a pejorative term, *queer* has been reclaimed by some LGBT people to describe themselves; however, it is not a universally accepted term, even within the LGBT community. When Q is seen at the end of LGBT, it may mean *queer* or *questioning*.

Questioning: A time in many people's lives when they question or experiment with their gender expression, gender identity, and/or sexual orientation. This experience is unique to everyone; for some, it can last a lifetime or be repeated many times over the course of a lifetime.

Sex: At birth, infants are commonly assigned a sex. This is usually based on the appearance of their external anatomy and is often confused with gender. However, a person's sex is actually a combination of bodily characteristics including chromosomes, hormones, internal and external reproductive organs, and secondary sex characteristics. As a result, there are many more sexes than just the binary male and female, just as there are many more genders than just male and female.

Sex reassignment surgery: See **Gender affirmation surgery**.

Sexual orientation: A person's enduring physical, romantic, and/or emotional attraction to another person. Gender identity and sexual orientation are not the same. Transgender people may be straight, lesbian, gay, bisexual, or queer. For example, a person who transitions from male to female and is attracted solely to men would typically identify as a straight woman.

Straight, or heterosexual: A word to describe women who are attracted to men and men who are attracted to women. This is not exclusive to those who are cisgender. For example, transgender men may identify as straight because they are attracted to women.

They/Them/Their: One of many sets of gender-neutral singular pronouns in English that can be used as an alternative to he/him/his or she/her/hers. Usage of this particular set is becoming increasingly prevalent, particularly within the LGBTQ community.

Transgender: An umbrella term for people whose gender identity and/or gender expression differs from what is typically associated with the sex they were assigned at birth. People under the transgender umbrella may describe themselves using one or more of a wide variety of terms—including transgender. A transgender identity is not dependent upon physical appearance or medical procedures.

Transgender man: People who were assigned female at birth but identify and live as a man may use this term to describe themselves. They may shorten it to *trans man*. Some may also use *FTM*, an abbreviation for *female-to-male*. Some may prefer to simply be called *men*, without any modifier. It is best to ask which term a person prefers.

Transgender woman: People who were assigned male at birth but identify and live as a woman may use this term to describe themselves. They may shorten it to *trans woman*. Some may also use *MTF*, an abbreviation for *male-to-female*. Some may prefer to simply be called *female*, without any modifier.

Transition: Altering one's birth sex is not a one-step procedure; it is a complex process that occurs over a long period of time. Transition can include some or all of the following personal, medical, and legal steps: telling one's family, friends, and co-workers; using a different name and new pronouns; dressing differently; changing one's name and/or sex on legal documents; hormone therapy; and possibly (though not always) one or more types of surgery. The exact steps involved in transition vary from person to person.

Transsexual: Someone who has undergone, or wishes to undergo, gender affirmation surgery. This is an older term that originated in the medical and psychological communities. Although many transgender people do not identify as transsexual, some still prefer the term.

BOOKS

Gromko, Linda, MD. *Where's MY Book?: A Guide for Transgender and Gender Non-Conforming Youth, Their Parents, & Everyone Else.* Bainbridge Books, 2015.

This book is intended to give gender nonconforming kids information they need to grow to be happy, productive, loving, and loved.

Storck, Kelly, and Grigni, Noah. *The Gender Identity Workbook for Kids: A Guide to Exploring Who You Are.* Oakland, CA: Instant Help, 2018.

A licensed clinical social worker, who specializes in gender nonconforming youth, offers real tools to help gender nonconforming kids thrive in all aspects of life.

Testa, Rylan Jay, and Coolhart, Deborah. *The Gender Quest Workbook: A Guide for Teens and Young Adults Exploring Gender.* Oakland, CA: Instant Help, 2015.

Comprehensive workbook that will help you navigate your gender identity and expression at home, in school, and with peers.

WEB SITES

gender spectrum. www.genderspectrum.org/groups/
Nonprofit providing resources and hosting online support groups for pre-teens, teens, parents, caregivers, and other family members.

GLAAD. www.glaad.org
National advocacy and education organization dedicated to advancing human rights for LGBTQ individuals through positive images in the media.

GLSEN. www.glsen.org
GLSEN (pronounced "glisten"), founded in 1990, is the leading national education organization focused on ensuring safe and affirming schools for LGBTQ students.

GSA Network. www.gsanetwork.org
Organization committed to fighting for educational justice by working with grassroots, youth-led groups, and GSAs, empowering them to educate their schools and communities, and advocate for just policies that protect LGBTQ youth from harassment and violence. Founded as the Gay–Straight Alliance Network in 1998, the group changed its name to Genders & Sexualities Alliance Network in 2016.

Human Rights Campaign. www.hrc.org
The largest national lesbian, gay, bisexual, transgender, and queer civil rights organization with more than 3 million members and supporters nationwide, HRC envisions a world where LGBTQ people are guaranteed their basic equal rights and can be open, honest, and safe at home, at work, and in the community.

It Gets Better Project. www.itgetsbetter.org
The nonprofit It Gets Better Project, founded in 2010, exists to uplift, empower, and connect LGBTQ youth around the globe. The Project includes more than 50,000 video messages from people of all sexual orientations, including many celebrities, reassuring young people who face bullying and harassment that life does, indeed, get better.

PFLAG. www.pflag.org
The nation's largest LGBTQ family and ally organization. Committed to advancing equality through its mission of support, education, and advocacy, PFLAG has 400 chapters and 200,000 supporters in major urban centers, small cities, and rural areas in all 50 states, the District of Columbia, and Puerto Rico.

Index

AUTHOR'S BIOGRAPHY

Anita R. Walker is a freelance writer based in Mississippi. Walker is a proud graduate of Copiah Lincoln Community College and Alcorn State University. She identifies as a pansexual female, while her daughter prefers a gender-neutral status. Walker lives in a small but diverse community of the Deep South. Walker is proud of her roots but strives to continue to broaden uneducated minds within her community.

CREDITS

COVER

(clockwise from top left) iStock; iStock/yacobchuk; iStock/justhavealook; iStock/Drazen

INTERIOR

1, shutterstock/ASDF_MEDIA; 3, shutterstock/Carolyn Dietrich; 11, shutterstock/qingqing; 12, shutterstock/Maksim Denisenko; 14, iStock/4x6; 15, iStock/katrinaelena; 17, iStock/sadeugra; 18, iStock/katrinaelena; 19, iStock/DGLimages; 21, iStock/Jbryson; 22, shutterstock/Anatoliy Karlyuk; 23, shutterstock/Sol Vazquez Cantero; 25, shutterstock/Sandratsky Dimitriy; 26, shutterstock/geartooth productions; 28, shutterstock/Oksana Ph; 30, iStock/isitsharp; 32, iStock/sturti; 33, iStock/RoBeDeRo; 34, iStock/CREATISTA; 35, iStock/Nicolas McComber; 36, iStock/Johnny Grieg; 37, iStock/funky-data; 39, iStock/reddees; 40, iStock/Nicolas McComber; 41, iStock/Beatriz Vera; 42, iStock/Nell Sidhoum; 44, iStock/awakenedeye; 46, iStock/GIGra; 47, iStock/powerofforever; 48, dreamstime/simplysel; 50, shutterstock/EvrenKalinbacak; 51, iStock/pidjoe; 53, iStock/Gökçen TUNÇ; 54, iStock/jedraszak; 56, iStock/tomeng; 57, shutterstock/Augustino; 58, shutterstock/VladOrlov; 60, shutterstock/kalcutta; 62, iStock/MStudioImages; 63, iStock/instants; 64, shutterstock/Ink Drop; 65, iStock/Nell Sidhoum; 67, shutterstock/FranciscoMarques; 68, iStock/REBEKANG; 69, shutterstock/Sk Hasan Ali; 70, shutterstock/Shane Meyers Photography; 71, shutterstock/arun sambha mishra; 72, shutterstock/tantrik71; 74, iStock/monkeybusinessimages; 75, iStock/fstop123; 76, iStock/juanmonino; 77, shutterstock/J. Bicking; 79, shutterstock/Monkey Business Images; 80, shutterstock/view apart; 83, iStock/JannHuizenga; 84, iStock/asiseeit; 85, iStock/fotostorm; 86, iStock/diane39; 88, shutterstock/Anna Demianenko